THE HOLY INFANT
OF PRAGUE

JOSEF FORBELSKÝ   JAN ROYT   MOJMÍR HORYNA

THE HOLY INFANT OF PRAGUE

PHOTOGRAPHS
by **KAREL** and **LADISLAV NEUBERT**

AVENTINUM

CONTENTS

THE HOLY INFANT
OF PRAGUE

THE SPIRITUAL TOUCH
OF THE ROMANIC WORLD

Mariano Picón Salas, an important Latin American writer, who in the 1930s lived in Prague as Venezuela's ambassador, left a permanent memory of his stay there in an essay called *The Czech Kingdom, the Kingdom of God*. This cultured intellectual did not fail to notice that the country in which he happened to find himself, and especially in its heart — Prague, hid under the secular layer spread all over Europe in modern times a strong spiritual tradition instilled by previous history. He felt the presence of the great drama of the Hussite and Lutheran Reformations, but as a Hispanic he also perceived, and expressed in a rich style, a powerful touch of the spiritual culture bequested to Bohemia by the Romanic countries and frequently brought over from Spain.

For the present visitor to the Czech metropolis this historical presence can be symbolized by the marble sarcophagus situated in the middle of the Gothic St Vitus' Cathedral, which next to Prague Castle towers above the city spread alongside the river Vltava. The sarcophagus is the last resting place of Emperor Ferdinand I, whose relief portrait it bears. The Emperor was a native of the Spanish town of Alcalá de Henares, famous for its humanist university and for another local celebrity, Miguel de Cervantes. In 1526 the Czech nobility elected Ferdinand I of the Hapsburg family King of Bohemia. Without fully realizing the fact, the inhabitants of this Central European country had by this act linked themselves in power to the area where the other branch of the same family reigned, which stretched from Bohemia across the Atlantic to as far as the Andes. King Ferdinand, administrator of the Czech, Hungarian and Austrian lands, had in his youth been brought up at the court of his grandparents, Ferdinand of Aragon and Isabella of Castile, the Catholic monarchs, in whose service thirty-four years before that, Christopher Columbus arrived at the shores of the New World. Ferdinand I was also brother to Emperor Charles V, for whom Hernán Cortés conquered the Aztec realm in 1521 and for whom, at the time of Ferdinand's election, Francisco Pizarro started the conquest of the Incas' empire.

With Ferdinand I's ascending the throne, Bohemia, in the 15th century plundered by the Hussite Wars and in the early 16th century excited by the rise of the Reformation, was not only influenced by the great power centred in the European Romanic Catholic south, but also became more exposed to the culture of Renaissance humanism and art, earlier hindered by the conflicts. The ruler, coming to Central Europe via the Netherlands, established relations with Erasmus of Rotterdam, and when he assumed his position on the throne, started to enrich the appearance of Prague by unrestrained Renaissance construction. The Royal Summer House and the nearby gardens still harmoniously embellish the area of Prague Castle and call to mind his efforts. At Ferdinand's court, often alternating between Vienna, Prague, and other prominent cities, a number of Spaniards appeared. A Renaissance poet Cristóbal de Castillejo, Ferdinand's friend from his younger years, whom the sovereign called to his service, was one of them. One of de Castillejo's most extensive poems of more than five thousand lines, depicting the benefits and troubles of court

Church of the Virgin Mary the Victorious in Malá Strana, viewed from Petřín

life, was dated in Prague, 1547. At that time, the culture of Spain literally entered Bohemia.

This was already the second year of the session of the Council of Trent in south Tyrol, which was to reform the Church which faced spreading Reformation. Spain was represented there by its great theologians and scholars, of whom the names of Melchor Cano and Domingo de Soto were preserved in history. The Spanish monarchy, during the 16th century recognized even by its critics and enemies as the greatest power of the time and a rightful inheritor of the Roman Empire (half a century before, it achieved victory in the 700-year-old fight against Islam), felt to be the guarantor of the religious orthodox creed. Therefore it was its task to transmit the stimuli of the Trent Council to the whole sphere of its influence.

In 1556 the Czech environment — at the

The Virgin Mary the Victorious, front of the church

time composed of a mixture of the old local Hussitism and the new Protestantism coming from the north of Germany — was first exposed to the influence of the Jesuit Order through the work of the Spaniard Ignatius of Loyola. His efforts, amalgamating the knightly ascetism with emphasis on the unpredestined character of spiritual fate, thus accentuating education and self-formation of the personality, were

Madonna on the front, 1644

Don Baltasar de Marradas' coat of arms on the front

aimed at schools and, in the form of various missions, also part of the popular strata of the inhabitants. The active spirituality was linked to efforts to renew the Catholicism of the Church: therefore some Czech and Moravian towns gradually became seats of splendid Jesuit colleges.

Reflecting in the sunshine, the gilt halo around the head of the statue of the Order's founder, erected above the Baroque church in the vicinity of the previous college, can still be seen in the New Town of Prague.

In a historian's words, the area of Bohemia became a cauldron in which various spiritual trends began melting: 'clashed,

intersected, merged and lasted longer than elsewhere. They welded as in the focus of a lens, and grew in intensity . . .'

Dynastic relations that established favourable conditions for this spread of south European spiritual culture to the centre of Europe were not limited to the figures of Emperors Charles V and Ferdinand I only. If we go back to the tomb in St Vitus' Cathedral, which was already mentioned, there are two other figures sculpted in the white stone next to Ferdinand: his wife Anne of Jagiello, for whom the unique Renaissance Summer House (Belvedere) near Prague Castle was built; and their son Maximilian II, the Czech, Ger-

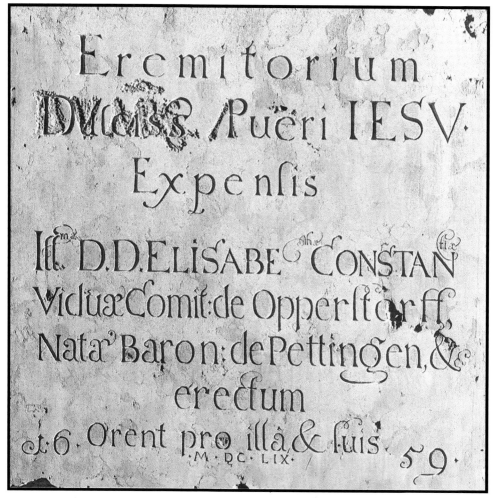

Foundation plaque from 1659 in the former hermitage of the Prague Holy Infant

man and Hungarian King and Emperor. When Maximilian was twenty-one, he went to Spain to marry Emperor Charles V's daughter Mary, his cousin, and there he made acquaintance with another of his cousins, the future co-ruler of the Hapsburg territories, Philip II. That same Philip II later acted as host and instructor to Maximilian's two sons, of whom Rudolf later attained the position of Emperor. He would choose Prague for his permanent seat and gathered there such remarkable personalities of art and science as, for example, Giuseppe Arcimboldo, Johannes Kepler, and Tycho de Brahe. Aetas Hispaniae, 'the Age of Spain', took hold in Central Europe as well.

One of the consequences of the dynastic

The Carmelite sign

The Maltese Knights' sign

relations between the south and centre of Europe was an intense diplomatic activity in which the aristocracy of both sides participated. Among the many Spanish envoys to the Emperor's court who tried to influence Central European politics at the turn of the 16th century when it was becoming rather entangled was Juan de Borja. In 1581 he had his own book printed in Prague, called *Empresas morales*, which contained interpretations of moralistic proverbs and principles; it was probably the first Spanish book printed in Prague.

The envoy Juan de Borja was the second son of Francisco de Borja, a Spanish grandee, who is said to have exchanged, under the impression of the view of the face of the deceased Emperor's wife, Isabella of Portugal, his life of a courtier for service in a Jesuit order. He was eventually sanctified, and nowadays a Praguer walking along the Gothic Charles Bridge can see the Baroque stone statue of him — St Francis Borgia. In Bohemia there is another reminder of this sanit: in 1958 a manuscript of the play *The Grand Duke of Gandia*, long considered lost, was found in one of the south Bohemian castles. The play was written by the illustrious Pedro Calderón de la Barca on the occasion of Francisco's canonization in 1671.

Another envoy of Spain, Guillermo de San Clemente, an educated Catalonian who received even Giordano Bruno in his residence, never returned to his native land. He was buried in 1608 in the Prague Church of St Thomas under the tombstone bearing his name.

The nobles of Bohemia and Moravia, mainly those of the Catholic minority, were likewise increasingly drawn into the stream of Spanish politics and the strong cultural and spiritual influences originating in the Iberian peninsula.

In 1548, as Maximilian was leaving Augsburg for Valladolid via Genoa and Barcelona for the journey to culminate the previously mentioned marriage to Emperor Charles V's daughter Mary, he was accompanied by several young Czech noblemen. Of these, eighteen-year-old Vratislav of Pernštejn, descendant of a prominent noble family, deserves the greatest attention. After he had proved his worth as Maximilian's envoy, he was sent to Italy in 1552. And it was probably at this time that his marriage to Doña María Manrique de Lara, daughter of Don García Manrique de Lara, was decided upon, a Spaniard serving Emperor Charles in Italy, and of Isabella de Bresegno, an Italian known for her links to the Neapolitan circle of the Erasmian follower Juan Valdés, and for this reason subjected to an Inquisitorial trial. The marriage of Vratislav and María was celebrated in September 1555. A year after that Vratislav of Pernštejn became Knight of the Golden Fleece, which was in appreciation of his diplomatic and political skills and merits. In later years he fulfilled other important missions; for example, in 1560 he represented Maximilian at the wedding of Philip II to Elizabeth of Valois. Through his service Vratislav was of good avail not only to his sovereign, but also to the Spanish Crown,

Rafael Sadeler, Dominic a Jesu Maria, copper engraving, around 1624

especially when in 1566 he became the Supreme Chancellor of the Czech Kingdom and a clever mediator between the Catholic and the Protestant nobilities. The Spanish king Philip II asked his envoy in Prague in 1571 to praise Pernštejn on his behalf for his proceedings, 'especially in religious matters', and thanked him for his loyalty. And Vratislav remained loyal to

Dominic a Jesu Maria, detail of the painting at the back of the church

Emperor Ferdinand II and Ferdinand III, King of Bohemia,
detail of the painting at the back of the church

Robert de Longin, copy of the picture of the Virgin Mary the Victorious in the High Altar, 1622

the Spanish king until his own death in 1582.

Vratislav's wife Doña María Manrique de Lara belonged to the ladies in waiting of Maximilian's wife María. With the arrival of María, the sister of the powerful Spanish king Philip II, at the imperial court, a kind of 'Spanish salon', a centre of Spanish social and cultural irradiation in Central Europe, was formed. And Vratislav's wife Doña María Manrique de Lara enhanced its influence.

When she still resided at the splendid Litomyšl castle in east Bohemia, she proved her religious zeal in the mostly non-Catholic environment by calling as missionaries to the large Pernštejn estates the first two Czech Jesuits, Šturm and Hostounský, direct pupils of Ignatius de Loyola. Also, her Prague mansion, in which she later lived, became a place of important meetings and visits. It was, for example, visited in 1578 by Antonio Possevino, an Italian Jesuit and missionary, who stayed in Prague at the time, and who was also famous for his journey to Moscow.

Although Doña María Manrique de Lara supported the efforts of the Jesuit Order in Bohemia and was in touch with its representatives, her devotion seems to have been most in tune with the inner Carmelite spirituality, the renewal and dissemination of which was then promoted by the indefatigable Theresa of Ávila. Doña María also agreed with her in her respect for the Holy Infant, whose sculpture she brought with her to Bohemia.

This Spanish lady of noble birth died in Prague in 1608. In Bohemia her portrait by Alonso Sánchez Coello has been preserved. In the painting Doña María with her right hand lightly embraces her little daughter Polyxena.

Out of the number of children born into the marriage of Vratislav of Pernštejn and Doña María Manrique de Lara, the daughter Polyxena assumed the most distinguished position, mainly because in 1587 she married Vilém of Rožmberk, a nobleman, who after the death of Vratislav of Pernštejn stood at the head of the pro-Spanish oriented aristocracy in Bohemia.

Vilém of Rožmberk promoted Spain's interests with such zeal that he was also made Knight of the Golden Fleece Order by the Spanish King Philip II. This important man's wife, Polyxena, received a very special wedding gift: her mother gave her the sculpture of the Holy Infant, a family palladium, which was a reflection of devotion in Doña María's home country and which had increasingly gained weight as a symbol of the new Baroque religious feeling in Bohemia.

Polyxena's marriage lasted five years. In 1603 this woman of outstanding sharpness of intellect and exceptional beauty entered a new matrimony, this time with Zdeněk Vojtěch of Lobkowicz. And again he was a nobleman of close links with the 'Spanish side'. Zdeněk Lobkowicz visited Spain several times, and during his first journey in 1589 he was even received by Philip II in his monumental seat — the Escorial, which only five years before had been finished by Juan de Herrera. The third Spanish trip of Zdeněk's was accomplished in 1598, the year in which King Philip II died in Escorial.

As the wife of Zdeněk, since 1599 the Supreme Chancellor of the Czech Kingdom, Polyxena experienced great political dramas that occurred at the beginning of the 17th century in Bohemia and that foreshadowed the European drama of the Thirty Years' War. In her home in Hradčany, Count Slavata, one of the victims of the Prague defenestration of 1618, found refuge and kind treatment.

Polyxena's husband Zdeněk Vojtěch of Lobkowicz died in 1628, eight years after the defeat of the Estates' Army at the White Mountain near Prague, where vic-

Marble sacred water basin, originally a baptizing font from the Lutheran Church of the Holy Trinity, around 1615

Church of the Virgin Mary the Victorious, interior

tory fell to the pro-Spanish part of the Czech nobility whose head he had been. With the support of the Spanish generals who participated in the battle, the church in Malá Strana (the Little Quarter) was finished and devoted to the Virgin Mary the Victorious. In the adjoining cloister the Order of the Barefooted Carmelites found their home in 1624, and it was to them that the widowed Polyxena of Lobkowicz bequested the sculpture, which since that time was not to belong as a safeguard to one family only, but to Prague, to Bohemia, to the world.

In the Czech Kingdom, carrying the cross of the bloodshed of the time, the celebrated figure of the Holy Infant in the care of the Carmelites was to become a symbol of a new beginning. It was to be a medium of a new devotion, of a spiritual flame that had been lit by the Spanish renewers of the Carmel tradition, St Theresa of Jesus and St John of the Cross.

The source of this flame was eventually embraced by the widowed Empress María who returned to Spain and made her permanent home in the Madrid convent of the Clare nuns (Descalzas Reales). Luisa and Jane, the daughters of Doña María Manrique de Lara who had brought the Holy

Chapel with the gracious Marian statue of 1626

Infant sculpture to Bohemia, also took refuge in the same place. Madrid at the time exhibited the power of the Empire and enjoyed the dazzling brilliance of the plays by Lope de Vega. These women seem to have shed their majestic status and noble birth at the feet of the Holy Infant: they preferred the world of ascetic devotion.

Josef Forbelský

PROLOGUE

When Rudolf II ascended the Czech throne in 1576, no one yet divined the dramatic circumstances under which the rule of this art-loving sovereign would end. Rudolf II assumed the position on the throne of a country which was a kingdom of 'two kinds of people' — the Protestant majority and the Catholic minority. Within the Protestants followers of John Calvin got the upper hand in the 16th century, whereas the traditional Utraquists were ousted to a less important position. The greatest defenders of the Catholic creed in Bohemia at this time included the ancient Czech noble families, as for example those of Lobkowicz, Martinic, Šternberk, and Pernštejn. They could get support for their political and religious views from foreigners from Italy and Spain, who acted as envoys of their countries to Rudolf's court, or who worked in his service. Especially influential were the envoys of Spain, representatives of the then strongest European power, where the Spanish branch of the Hapsburg family ruled. Some of the prominent Czech noblemen confirmed their loyalty to 'facción española' by marriages to noblewomen of Spanish families.

The bleak religious situation was also reflected in the absence of new churches and convents. More often, the old mediaeval sacred constructions were being renovated and modified. Exceptions to this rule were, for example, a small Church of St Roche in Strahov, which was built by Rudolf II to commemorate the end of the plague in a style reminiscent of the Gothic, some buildings belonging to the Jesuits (in Bohemia since 1556), and also to the Protestants, as for example, in 1609 the Church of St Saviour in the Old Town.

In Malá Strana (the Little Quarter) as well, the Lutherans and the Calvinists had their congregations. In 1584 one of them built a chapel which, according to sources, was called by the name of Master Jan Hus, or that of St John the Baptist. The Meissen wood-carver Samuel Lorenz made an altarpiece for the chapel called The Last Supper. In 1599 a hospital was built in the vicinity of the chapel. The small size of the chapel was no longer adequate for the needs of the growing congregation. On July 20, 1611, several months after the invasion of Prague by the mercenary army of the Passau bishop and after Rudolf II had stepped down and Emperor Matthias had been installed, the foundation stone to a new church was laid. Many prominent Protestants participated in the occasion, above all Heinrich Mates, the count of Thurn, Linhart Colonna of Fels, and the predicants Matěj Höe and Elias Šúd. On July 26, 1613, after a sermon called 'The Eight Reasons For Which God Finally Granted Religious Freedom to This Kingdom', the church, whose total cost was 62 thousand Rhenish guilders, was dedicated under the name of the Holy Trinity. This dedication, the same as that of St Saviour, is the most frequent in Protestant chapels and it corresponded to the consecration of the Church of Santa Trinita dei Monti in Rome, after whose model the Prague church was built. It is slightly ironical that the Baroque style, in Bohemia usually linked with the Catholic Counter-Reformation, entered Bohemia in the form of a Lutheran church. The interior of the church was in the Lutheran spirit, which means very simple. The entrance was where today there is the altar of the

Talmberk Chapel

Prague Holy Infant. The altar of the Last Supper, moved over here from the older Church of Master Jan Hus, was situated at the back in the east, which is where the present front is. The vaulted ceiling of the church was decorated with a picture of the Holy Trinity. Out of the former Lutheran church, however, only the baptizing font is extant today, and it serves as sacred water basin.

THE VIRGIN MARY
THE VICTORIOUS

On May 23, 1618, an event occurred which foreshadowed the history of the Lands of the Czech Crown. The participants of a meeting of the estates, who were Eucharistic, proceeded to Prague Castle and from the windows of the Chancery threw out the governors Vilém Slavata of Chlum and Košumberk, and Jaroslav Bořita of Martinic, who were considered the main adversaries of the political and religious efforts of the Protestants. Both nobles were almost miraculously saved and reported the event to the Emperor in Vienna. This was the beginning of one of the most horrible wars that afflicted Bohemia — the Thirty Years' War. The fortune of the war alternated beween the two sides. Emperor Ferdinand II allied with the Bavarian Elector Maximilian and the Saxon Elector and Protestant John George of Saxony. The Czech Protestant relied on the recently elected Czech King Friedrich of Pfalz (Frederick of the Palatinate), who had relatives in the Protestant world, especially in England, but were eventually left to their own devices in their struggle.

At Emperor Ferdinand II's wish the Carmelite General (1617—20) Dominic a Jesu Maria (1559—1630), a Spaniard by birth, left for Munich accompanied by a brother in the order, Pietro della Madre di Dio, and joined Tilly and Charles Bonaventura Buquoy's army approaching Prague via south Bohemia. In a Johannite cloister in Strakonice that had been confiscated by the Czech Estates in 1619, Dominic a Jesu found a small (28.5 by 17.5 cm) late Gothic panel painting of the adoration of Christ, in which the Virgin Mary, St Joseph and the shepherds had their eyes plucked out. The two Carmelites took the picture and followed the army as far as the White Mountain.

On November 8, 1620, a battle was fought in which the Protestants seemed to be more fortunate, especially thanks to the effort of the cavalry of Prince Christian of Anhalt, Jr. The cavalry launched a successful attack on the regiment of the Spanish General Marradas, led by the Colonel Felipe de Areyçaga y Avendano. The Catholic army, with the white stripes on their hats and with the slogan Sancta Maria, responded with their own attack, while, according to a legend (Fr. Beckovský), Dominic a Jesu Maria blessed them with the Strakonice painting. Without doubt, he and the Irish Jesuit Henry Fitzsimont, the confessor of Count Buquoy, administered the Host to the soldiers before the battle. The Battle of the White Mountain, whose drama ended at the walls of the Star Summer House (Hvězda), practically meant the end of the Protestants' influence in the country. The 'Winter King' Frederick of the Palatinate, who had not taken part in the battle, fled the country. The victory over the 'Czech pagans' was extensively celebrated. Ferdinand II issued a medal on this occasion made by Pietro de Pomis. It emphasized, in the symbol of God's right hand — 'dextera Dei' — holding the imperial crown, and in the inscription (Dextera Domini fecit virtutem), the legitimacy of imperial power and its higher sanctification. The papal nuncio in Vienna, Carlo Caraffa, called Ferdinand a 'new Constantin'; the papal legate Verospi celebrated him as 'vicarius Christi'. A similarly triumphant tone sounded in the sermon by Ferdinand's confessor, the Belgian Jesuit Wilhelm La-

St Theresa of Ávila altar

mormaini, who called upon the Emperor for a merciless revenge on the rebels.

In the writings of this period a considerable share of the victory is ascribed to the Virgin Mary the Victorious. References were made to similar help by the Mother of God to Don Juan de Austria, in the Battle of Lepanto where the Turkish fleet was destroyed. At the White Mountain where the battle had been fought, a construction of the Servite monastery and the Church of the Virgin Mary the Victorious was set upon in 1627; the project was later abandoned. Only in the first decade of the 18th century the idea of making the White Mountain, where so far only a small chapel stood, into a place of pilgrimages came into focus again. The famous Czech Baroque architect Giovanni Santini took up the construction and in 1708—12 built a church on a cross plan, surrounded by ambulatories. The victory of the White Mountain was celebrated in 1728 by a Bavarian painter Cosmas Damian Asam in a painting called *The Victorious Church* in the central cupola of the temple. In the south cupola there is a painting by Czech Baroque painter Václav Vavřinec Reiner with the subject of Father Dominic praying at the head of the Imperial Army. The victorious tone is also noticeable in literature depicting the White Mountain as a place of pilgrimages.

The subsequent history of the picture of the Virgin Mary of Strakonice (the Victorious) is very rich. Together with the banners taken from the adversary at the White Mountain, it was brought to Rome, where in a ceremonial procession it was handed over to the Pope and exhibited in the Church of St Maria Maggiore; but on that same day it was transferred to St Paul's Church of the Barefooted Carmelites on the Quirinal, which was later consecrated to the Virgin Mary the Victorious. Emperor Ferdinand II had the picture adorned with a gold crown, the cost of which had also been contributed to by the suppressed Prague citizens. The celebrations linked with the transfer of the painting to Rome are described in a piece of writing called *Relazione della processione e festa fatte in Roma . . . nel collare l'imagine della Madona della Victoria nella chiesa de Paolo* (Rome 1622), which was also published in German by J. Ulr. Schoenigk in Augsburg, in 1622. In 1853 the picture was burnt in a fire in the church and it was replaced by a copy, the cost of which was paid by Prince A. Torlonio.

The first copy of the Strakonice picture was made as early as 1622 in Rome by the painter Robert de Longin. It was presented to the Carmelites of the Church of the Virgin Mary the Victorious in Malá Strana, where we can still see it in the upper part of the High Altar. The second copy, which was provided with a detailed Czech inscription, dates from the mid-17th century and it was commissioned for the side altar of the Johannite church in Strakonice. It was paid for by the Literate Brotherhood and brought to the church in a famous procession on June 26, 1650. According to the testimony of the Jesuit Bohuslav Balbín, a distinguished Czech Baroque historian (*Diva montis sancti*, 1655, p. 162), the painting was copied in Strakonice in 1653 by the painter Jan Schnabel. The third copy, painted on canvas in 1708, at the expense of Pavel Hager and provided with signs of its authenticity, was in 1709 cere-

St John of the Cross altar

monially placed in the High Altar of the new Church of the Virgin Mary the Victorious at the White Mountain. Another interesting thing is that the Johannites had a copy made for their Church of the Virgin Mary under the Chain. Besides other things, the reason must have been that the Order recalled the Christian victory at Lepanto, or in the Maltese siege, both of which were said to have been achieved with the support and help from the Virgin Mary — as we can also see in the painting by Karel Škréta in the High Altar of the church. The White Mountain picture was also reminiscent of the fact that in 1784 the Johannites took over the Church of the Virgin Mary the Victorious, and that Dominic a Jesu Maria found the original picture in a Johannite monastery in Strakonice. The White Mountain picture was reproduced in numbers by both painted copies and prints (by e.g. A. Birkhart, M. J. Rentz, J. J. Balzer, and others), they were applied to the façades of houses as house signs (Prague, Malá Strana, No. 160/IV), and in plastic form to the commemorative plague column (Hostivice near Prague), and even to the ambulatories of pilgrimage places. The respect given to the picture of the Virgin Mary the Victorious can also be recognized in that the last male descendant of the Czech Slavata noble family, Charles, Count of Slavata, since 1721 the General of the Order of the Barefooted Carmelites in Rome, had a copy made for the Spanish Queen María, which today can be found in Jindřichův Hradec in south Bohemia. The interesting thing is that it has not been mentioned in writings dedicated to miraculous pictures adored throughout Europe, for example in Gumpenberg's *Atlas Marianus*.

THE BAREFOOTED CARMELITES
AND THE CHURCH
OF THE VIRGIN MARY
THE VICTORIOUS

For reasons of a political alliance between the Czech King and German Emperor Ferdinand and the Elector John George of Saxony, the Lutheran service in the Church of the Holy Trinity continued even after the Battle of the White Mountain. It was only in 1622 that the last Lutheran predicant had to leave the temple and for a short time the church remained closed.

In Vienna, Ferdinand II promised Dominic a Jesu to establish two cloisters for the Barefooted Carmelites in memory of the White Mountain victory. He founded the first one in Vienna in 1623. In Prague, the Emperor gave the Carmelites the Church of the Holy Trinity, on condition that it would be consecrated to the Virgin Mary the Victorious and to St Anthony of Padua.

The Carmelite Order originated in the Holy Land, and its name derives from Mount Carmel, praised by Jews and pagans alike as the Lord's garden. As legend holds, the Virgin Mary herself visited this blessed place when still among living people. The prophets Elijah and Eliseus stayed there and built a chapel, around which many hermits, who wanted to follow their ascetic way of life, found their abode in caves. Gradually this community evolved into a Carmelite Order, which in 1209 was approved by St Albert, the Jerusalem Patriarch. From the order, which in the 1350s settled in Bohemia (at the Church of the Virgin Mary of the Snows in Prague), in 1568 a reformed and stricter branch of the so-called Barefooted Carmelites (Ordo Carmelitarum Discalceatorum) separated. The reform of the order had started in Spain in 1567 by St Theresa of Ávila, and it was complemented by St John of the Cross. The separation of this stricter observance was approved by Pope Clement VIII in 1593. The order pledged to remain in poverty and to observe strict fasts (they were not allowed to eat meat at all), and to keep silence from vespers until the morning service of the next day. According to the rules, the members of the order were to live in separate hermitages, but in Prague this idea had to be abandoned.

Ferdinand II presented the members of the order with a house on the south side of the church, originally inhabited by the Protestant predicant, and with a church-yard, on the premises of which there was a chapel of St John, newly consecrated to St Louis and since 1623 serving the French. The Spanish General Don Martín de Huerta bought the Carmelites the adjoining house (which today houses the Ministry of Education of the Czech Republic) for 9,000 guilders.

On September 7, 1624, the General Vicar Kašpar Arsenius of Radbuza led the way for the Carmelites into the former Lutheran church, which on the next day was consecrated by the apostolic visitant of the Minorites, Jan Savonanti, to the Virgin Mary the Victorious and to St Anthony of Padua. By the end of October 1624 the first Carmelites had arrived from Vienna. The members of the order, who in their famous pledge postulated that they would live on alms only, refused the grant of Emperor Ferdinand II. A noviciate was established at the cloister, which was moved over to Munich in 1630. The adverse economic situation of the cloister made the Emperor order the Czech Royal Chamber to pay the cloister 2,000 guilders a year. During the

Picture of the Virgin Mary of Mantua in the altar of St John of the Cross

Relief with the legend of the Virgin Mary of Mantua picture, detail of the frame

invasion of Prague by the Saxon Commander Arnheim in 1631 most of the members of the order left the city and a Protestant preacher Jan Rosacius Hořovický started to deliver sermons there. On May 15, 1632, the imperial General Albrecht of Wallenstein drove the Saxon army out of Prague and the Carmelites could come back to their home cloister. In 1633 the Emperor's contribution to the cloister was withdrawn and when, on top of that in 1634, the noviciate was reinstituted, the community soon became poor again. Once more the Carmelites had to flee — from the Swedish army of General Banner in 1634, and they could return only after General Colloredo

Pulpit, around 1680

Prophet Elijah, sculpture by J. L. Scheiermann, 1679, detail viewed from the pulpit

rebuffed the Swedish attack. The cloister faced .danger again in 1648 when the Swedes invaded Prague, but the Swedish army leader Königsmark, at the instance of some persons partial to the Carmelites, issued a protective warrant. The Protestant service was reintroduced to the church, and a hospital was established in the clois-ter. After the Thirty Years' War the cloister recovered from the war devastation and the subsequent plague. In 1710 forty Carmelites lived there, most of whom came from the German lands, but here were also Italians and Spaniards. A large amount of income was constituted by the production of Carmelite water from balm

St Simon Stock altar, around 1670

(*aqua aromatica melissae*), which had reached such proportions that the Carmelites had to reserve the whole wing of the monastery for it. This medicine, used especially in cases of paralysis, had been invented by a French Carmelite from the Paris cloister in rue de Vaugirard, who had settled in the Trent monastery and handed the secret down to other brethren in the order.

The Carmelites' activity at the Church of the Virgin Mary the Victorious was ended by an Imperial decree of June 3, 1784. The property of the cloister was confiscated and given to the religious administration. On the grounds a tax office and a grammar school were established. The Carmelite vineyards went to the general seminary. In the garden house in the middle of Petřín hill slope, which belonged to the cloister garden, there was a painting depicting St Elijah in a chariot of fire, and in the rocks there were several little caves with the Holy Infant pictures.

After the abolition of the cloister, the Church of the Virgin Mary the Victorious became a parish church. The parsonage was moved here from the nearby Church of the Virgin Mary under the Chain and the spiritual administration was entrusted to the priests of the Order of Maltese Knights.

THE PRAGUE HOLY INFANT

Nothing made the Prague Church of the Virgin Mary the Victorious so famous in the world as the small, 47 cm high wax sculpture of the Holy Infant, called the Gracious Holy Infant (Gratiosus Iesulus). Its cultic significance was explained in a booklet *Pragerisches Gross und Klein* written in German in 1736 by Prior Emerich a S. Stephano and translated into Czech in 1749.

The cult of Christ's childhood (Infantia Christi) has a thousand-year-old tradition in the Catholic Church. Besides the texts of the Gospels, the artists depicting Christ's childhood used as their sources apocryphal texts, mainly James' and Thomas' pseudo-gospels. God in the small child was adored by Holy Fathers and writers, for example St Athanasius (d. 373) and St Jerome (d. 420) who spent 34 years of his life as a hermit in the vicinity of the Saviour's birthplace. The small Jesus was greatly respected by St Bernard of Clairvaux (d. 1153), St Francis of Assisi (d. 1226), who during a miracle in Grecio beheld the newly born Christ, and miracle-inducer St Anthony of Padua (d. 1231), who is usually depicted with the Holy Infant in his arms. In the Baroque period St Theresa of Ávila belonged to the worshippers of the Holy Infant, and she would not set out on a journey without her sculpture of him. In Bethlehem, Emperor Constantine built a basilica above Christ's birthplace, and monuments commemorating Christ's childhood were later worshipped in many temples of Byzantine Empire and western Europe. The centre of this cult was the Church of St Maria Maggiore in Rome.

Isolated depiction of the Holy Infant outside the usual scenes has appeared since the early 14th century. The oldest sculptures can be found in Germany, where the representative image had formed in the visionary environment of women's convents. Similar to most of the other German 'Andachtsbilder' (for example the Pieta, the group of Christ and John the Evangelist, the Virgin Mary in childbed, and others), which originated in the same period, it has also its roots in spiritual poetry. Especially in the 15th century, the Holy Infant was usually rendered with all details, and the naturalistic effect was often enhanced with polychromy. The standing, less often sitting, child usually holds various objects in his hands. Most frequently he blesses with his left hand, and in the right one he holds either a bird, an apple, a sphere, a book, a cross or a bunch of grapes, which is either a reference to the Eucharist, or an allegory of Christ, according to St John's Gospel (John 15, 1-11). There are also instances of the small Holy Infant being taken out of the abdomen of the Virgin Mary (Mater gravida) sculpture at Christmas, which was then wrapped in blankets and laid in a decorative manger, or cradle, such as is extant in the Bayerisches Nationalmuseum (mid-14th century). Since the early Middle Ages it became customary to dress the sculptures. For example, in the inventory of the Břevnov Monastery dating to 1390-94, there is a record of a pluvial and a mitre of St Vojtěch (Adalbert), and a similar account of the dress for the Virgin Mary. The mediaeval fabrics are only rarely extant, though. One of the few exceptions is the clothes of the Holy Infant of Mechelen (Schwerin Museum), which, same as the sculpture, comes from around 1500.

High Altar, 1723

The oldest known sample of the Holy Infant is a 28 cm high sculpture of a Holy Infant blessing with a bird in his right hand from the 1340s, in the Mödingen Monastery near Dillingen (the present Maria-Medingen). One of the most beautiful sculptures, mainly thanks to the well-preserved polychromy, is the Holy Infant with a bunch of grapes in Bayerisches Nationalmuseum in Munich, carved around 1462 by the Master of Dangolsheimer Madonna. There are more 'Andachtsbilder' illustrating widespread respect for Jesus' childhood already in the Middle Ages: e.g. the motif of the Holy Infant being taught to walk by angels (Bayerisches Nationalmuseum, around 1480). Lucas Cranach the Elder often rendered the Holy Infant in his paintings, frequently with a cross in his hand (e.g. the National Gallery in Prague, around 1534). A famous depiction is that of a Holy Infant in the heart in the middle of Arma Christi, in the engraving by Master E. S. dating from 1467. In the 16th century the motifs of Christ's childhood appear especially in engravings, printed in the Netherlands by the Wierix family, and in the 17th − 18th centuries in Bohemia by the Birkhart family.

The cult of Christ's childhood gained in importance in the Baroque period when it was mainly linked with the visions of the Spanish St Theresa of Ávila. A number of sculptures of the Holy Infant from that time can be found in Spain, and one of those, as we already know, got as far as Prague. In Rome the divine child was likewise given its due respect, especially in the temple of St Maria Aracoeli on the Capitol, where a wooden sculpture of Santo Bambino has been kept since 1629. It comes from the Holy Land where the Franciscans carved it from olive wood from the Gethsemane garden at the end of the 15th century.

In the Austrian lands, the most famous was the Holy Infant worshipped by the Capuchins in Salzburg. It is 11.5 cm in height and was carved from ivory; in its right hand it holds a cross, and a sceptre in its left. A number of sculptures were worshipped in the capital of the monarchy, Vienna. The Prague Carmelite Holy Infant of Malá Strana was not left alone, either. In the Cyriacian Monastery of the Holy Rood the Greater, in the Old Town of Prague, a sculpture 'Pueri Iesu Gratiosi' was revered, similar to that in Salzburg, but holding the cross in both hands.

Unlike the mediaeval Holy Infant sculptures that had been carved from wood, the Baroque ones were also made of wax, ivory and bronze, sometimes even of papier-mâché. The Baroque sculptures were all dressed in garments imitating the aristocratic fashion of the period, but Holy Infants dressed in peasant clothes are known as well.

In Bohemia, no exact sculpture of the Holy Infant is known before the Baroque period. Relying on reports, we can only assume that depictions of this sort had existed here, too − evidence being in the wall paintings from the 14th century in the capitular hall of the Sázava Monastery, where there is a beautiful motif of Infantia Christi.

The cult of the Holy Infant in Bohemia developed fully only in the Baroque period, and the Prague sculpture was its most important agent. Its origin is still surrounded by mystery. It probably comes

St Joseph altar, around 1670

from a monastery that was situated between Cordoba and Seville, and it is a copy of a wooden sculpture worshipped in that place. From there it was obtained by Doña Isabella Manrique de Lara y Mendoza. She then gave it as a wedding gift to her daughter María Manrique de Lara who married one of the most prominent nobles of the Czech Kingdom, Vratislav of Pernštejn. The Holy Infant sculpture became a wedding gift also in the case of the marriage of María's daughter Polyxena to another important nobleman of the Czech Kingdom, Vilém of Rožmberk (1587). Polyxena brought the Holy Infant even to her next marriage — this time to the Supreme Chancellor of the Czech Kingdom, Zdeněk Vojtěch of Lobkowicz. After Vojtěch's death in 1628, when Polyxena moved to live in the castle of Roudnice nad Labem, she presented the sculpture to the Order of the Barefooted Carmelites at the Church of the Virgin Mary the Victorious in Malá Strana. Since then a well known history of the Prague Holy Infant has evolved, accompanied by many supplications and miracles. As the legend goes, the Lady Polyxena gave the sculpture to the Carmelites, saying: 'I am giving you what I most esteem of my possessions; keep the sculpture in reverence, and you will be well off.' The Prior of the monastery P. Ludvík placed the Holy Infant in the oratory where it was mostly worshipped by the novices. The members of the order ascribed then the subsequent improvement in the financial situation of the monastery to the Holy Infant (but the improvement was also caused by the decree of Emperor Ferdinand II).

In 1630 the novices left for Munich and the worship of the Holy Infant decreased. In 1631 the Saxons invaded Prague, and besides other things, they also plundered the Carmelite cloister. Prior Ignaz returned there in 1632 when the Saxons had been driven away, but did not renew the worship of the Holy Infant. In 1633 all the financial support of the Crown to the cloister was suspended. Some saw in it a punishment for the irreverence to the sculpture of the 'Little Praguer'. In 1634 Prior P. Felician a S. Bartholomeo had to flee again, this time from the Swedes. The Holy Infant sculpture was found again only in 1638, by P. Cyril a Matre Dei, who came to Prague at Whitsuntide of 1637. He came from Luxembourg and his civil name was Nicholas Schockwilerg. As the sculpture had its arms broken off, they had to be replaced; they were made of wood coated with wax and were paid for by a retired army commissioner. Even at the time the Holy Infant sculpure had been linked to a number of miracles, which, together with the later ones, were recorded in the book by P. Emerich a S. Stephano. Many supplicants turned to the Holy Infant during the Swedish siege of Prague in the years 1639 and 1641. The sculpture was revered by the Czech nobility, which was reflected in a number of financial gifts to the cloister. The legend of the miraculous Holy Infant sculpture was so widespread that the Carmelites decided to exhibit it so that the general public could worship it too. According to a decision in 1641, the sculpture was to be placed in the still existing chapel of the Holy Rood, next to the entrance of the church on the left. But the decision was realized only thirteen years later when the chapel had been finished at the expense of

Prague Holy Infant altar, 1776

the Lords of Talmberk. In 1647 Emperor Ferdinand III himself prayed before the Holy Infant, and as an expression of gratitude presented the church with forty large wax candles. The Lady Febronia of Pernštejn was a great worshipper of the sculpture and she had a marble floor laid in the temple, and provided the High Altar with a life-size crucifix. In 1644 she bequested the Holy Infant part of her estate. At the same time Lady Polyxena Slavata presented the church with an altar of St Simon Stock, John Conrad of Altendorf had the altar of St Joseph established, and the Count and Countess Kolowrat gave the Holy Infant a silver curtain, a lamp, and a reliquary; Lady Brunetti even established a foundation of 1,000 Rhenish guilders for the eternal light at the Holy Infant's altar.

During the Swedish invasion of Prague the church with the Holy Infant was saved from the plundering soldiers because, as was mentioned before, the Swedish General Königsmark issued a protective warrant requested by the Carmelites on the advice of Colonel Kappy. It was also due to the merit of the soldier Ruttger, a former pupil of the Carmelites in Cologne. The Swedes established a hospital in the convent, and Charles Gustav, later the Swedish King, gave the Holy Infant thirty ducates when visiting it.

The Lords of Martinic were great supporters of the Holy Infant. They prompted the procession of January 14, 1651, that carried the sculpture from the Church of the Virgin Mary the Victorious to other Prague temples. During these ceremonies the Holy Infant acquired the attribute of Gracious (Gratiosus) and it was presented with a little gold crown from Bernard Ignatius of Martinic, and crowned by him, as well. Four years later, on April 4, 1655, an even more solemn coronation of the Holy Infant took place. Bernard Ignatius of Martinic had a gold crown made for the occasion, set with precious stones and pearls. As the archbishop Cardinal Harrach III was ill, the task of the coronation was entrusted into the hands of the suffragan P. Josef Corta, Archbishop of Sebastya, but the crown had not been sanctified by the Pope, as was prescribed for the ceremony of the Marian pictures' coronation (e.g. the one in Svatá Hora near Příbram, in 1732). To commemorate the conferment of the Order of the Golden Fleece by the Spanish King, the Count Bernard Ignatius of Martinic had a smaller copy made to be hung on the Holy Infant's neck. Judging from the memorial plaque set inside the chapel, Elizabeth Constance of Pötting had a 'hermitage for the sweet boy Jesus' made for the Holy Infant sculpture in 1659. This tower-like structure, as rendered to us faithfully by Folpert of Ouden-Allen in his prospectus of 1680-85, was built behind the temple on the left, next to the outer wall of the convent. In a copy of the old plans, kept in the parsonage of the Church of the Virgin Mary the Victorious, the hermitage bears the name of 'Exercitien-Haus'. The Carmelites called the hermitage 'eremitorium dulcissimi pueri Iesu'. In 1733 an unknown thief stole the orb, and probably also the Order of the Golden Fleece, from the sculpture.

The Prague Holy Infant became famous throughout Europe thanks to the mentioned book by P. Emerich a S. Stephano, published in German in 1736 and in Czech

Glazed case with the sculpture of the Prague Holy Infant

in 1749. In the chapter dedicated to miracles, the sculptor Jan Jiří Schlansovský is mentioned, who around 1739 made a copy of the Holy Infant in three sizes. He carved about a hundred sculptures which travelled to countries all over Europe. Greater popularity of the Holy Infant was also ensured by a series of holy pictures made by prominent Czech Baroque engravers, for example A. Birkhart and M. J. Rentz; many were coloured by hand. Not all of them met the strict criteria of censorship, though. In 1769 Empress Maria Theresa ordered a confiscation of 110 small engravings by a miniaturist: in the inscription below the engraving the Holy Infant was compared to Alexander the Great, as both were short. Important and miraculous events linked with the Holy Infant are depicted in a series of 18th-century pictures to be found on the grounds of the church.

As the tight space of the chapel did not match the flood of pilgrims, the general visitant of the order P. Ildefons a Praesentatione B.V.M. transferred on January 13, 1741, the sculpture of the Holy Infant to the side altar of SS Joachim and Anne, opposite the miraculous picture of the Virgin Mary of Mantua. The older altarpiece was replaced with a glazed case made of drawn silver by the famous Packeni family from Malá Strana. In the course of the ceremony the sculpture was decorated with the so-called prostholet, a bracelet made by the Prague goldsmith Hachtle from jewels given to the Holy Infant by various ladies, for example Maria Theresa Scheffler, the Princess of Taxis, and the noble Lady Vřesovec. The bracelet was priced at 5,000 guilders. In 1741, after Emperor

Charles VI died, Prague was invaded by the armies of Bavarian Elector Karl Albert who got himself crowned as Czech King. Fortunately, not much damage was done to Prague, and as a gesture of gratitude, a public collection was organized out of which the Holy Infant acquired a large silver ball with an engraved chronograph of this wording: 'AnatheMa, qVod praeserVata Pragensis CIVItas GratIoso IesVLi eXoLVIt' (a gift by the preserved city of Prague to the Gracious Holy Infant). Next to the glazed case receptacles for oblations were installed. The grateful donors — the people who regained their health at the Holy Infant's intercession — placed miniature silver limbs in there. As in other pilgrimage temples throughout Bohemia, these were removed at the time of the Josephine reforms. A graceful ex voto with a figure of the Holy Infant was painted, out of gratitude for the preservation of his family during the Bavarian occupation of Prague by the painter Jan Jiří Schmidt from Malá Strana. In 1776 a new altar was established for the Holy Infant case. The architecture of the piece made of Czech marble was the work of the Prague stonecutter František Lauermann, and the wooden gilt polychromous sculptures of the Virgin Mary and St Joseph were made by Petr Prachner. The altar was consecrated on December 26, 1776, by the Maltese Knight Fra Jan Raymund.

After the death of Maria Theresa, herself a great advocate of the Holy Infant, her son Joseph II ascended the throne, and he abolished the Carmelite cloister on July 3, 1784. The parsonage of the Maltese Knights was moved to the church, and they became new keepers of the Holy Infant

SS Joachim and Anne altar, around 1670

sculpture. The state of things was adverse, and there was not enough money to repair the temple. The bad condition of the altar of the Prague Holy Infant nevertheless required some restoration and the parson Jan Slánský entrusted the stonecutter P. Ciani and the guilder J. Nejtek with the task. The repair costs were 776 gold coins. To cover these, according to records in the Memorial Book, the Holy Infant had to tour other Prague churches with a 'beggar's bag'. In August 1879 it was exhibited at the Merciful Sisters' in Bartolomějská Street, in October and November at the Merciful Sisters of St Charles of Boromeo below Petřín hill, it spent several days in the Sacré Coeur convent in Smíchov, and for some time it visited the English Virgins and Elizabethans. In the 19th century the fame of the Prague Holy Infant spread to the Spanish-speaking countries of South America and to Italy. The English Virgins in the Rhine region and the Augustinians in Paris prayed a special officium as a homage to it. The Prague Holy Infant was famous all over the Hapsburg Empire and in Bavaria. In 1928 a celebration of the 300th anniversary of the gift of the Holy Infant to the Carmelites was held in the Church of the Virgin Mary the Victorious, with many important guests participating in it. The Bolivian Embassy had a mass served in the Church of the Virgin Mary the Victorious on the day of the anniversary of the foundation of their state. The Philippines were grateful for much help from the Holy Infant as well.

The sculpture of the Prague Holy Infant, as we already mentioned in the introduction, is 47 cm high (including the 2 cm base). To protect it from damage, it is loosely set in a silver case in the shape of truncated cone reaching up to its waist. The sculpture probably has a wooden core sheathed in fabric that can be seen through the wax. The Holy Infant is not naked, as was the case with the mediaeval sculptures in Germany, but the wax sculptor modelled a long shirt (kolobion) around his body, a similar one to that known from the pictures of Madonnas of Eastern provenance. In its features, the face of the child gives away its Spanish origin.

The sculpture of the Prague Holy Infant has always been dressed. According to reports it was first dressed by Anna Loragh and Marie Sibylla Schayemaier, and since 1747 by the English Virgins. The Holy Infant used to wear a white gown, a white robe, and a silk garment similar to a dalmatic over it. The fourth and fifth robes, beautifully embroidered and adorned, were reminiscent of a priest's pluvial. The head of the Holy Infant was decorated with gilt crowns, one of which dates from 1767 and the other from 1810-20. Its wardrobe is very rich: there are almost sixty pieces of clothing. The oldest comes from 1700. In 1754 the Holy Infant was presented with a beautifully embroidered dress by Maria Theresa. A number of dresses were given by the devotees from far-away Asia, for example from a village Tou-se-we near Shanghai (1894), from the Philippines, and from Vietnam. The Holy Infant was also given presents from other parts of the world, especially from South and North America, and from a number of European countries.

The fame of the Holy Infant was spread through copies touched by the original. Porcelain copies were made in Meissen

Petr Brandl's painting, The Prayer of SS Joachim and Anne, detail, around 1716

Coats of arms on the ceiling of the nave

*Lady Polyxena of Lobkowicz handing the Prague Holy Infant sculpture over to the Carmelites,
painting from the first half of the 18th century*

from a model made by the sculptor Gottlieb Kirchner. The mold that was preserved in Meissen was later repaired by the famous modeller J. J. Kandler. Copies of the Prague Holy Infant were placed in nearly all the Malá Strana churches, e.g. in St Thomas', in the Church of the Virgin Mary under the Chain, and in all the cloisters and churches under the Carmelite administration throughout Bohemia (in St Havel's in Prague, in Skuhrov, in Solnice, Uhřínov, and other places). In St Joseph's Church in the Prague Malá Strana a sculpture was kept of the Holy Infant, presented by the Lady of Textor in 1737. Since 1722 the sculpture of the Holy Infant has been worshipped in the Prague Church of the Elizabethans Na slupi. In return for saving her life, the Prioress of the convent had an altar built for the Holy Infant in 1739. The sculpture was then ceremoniously touched by the Carmelite P. Anthony in 1740. A copy of the Holy Infant also stood in the now abolished Church of St Anne in the Old Town of Prague. In Plzeň (Pilsen), the church of the Prague Holy Infant was built by the Mayor Petr Pavel Helffer in 1746. Altars with sculptures of the Prague Holy Infant can be found in Hořín near Mělník, in Chocerady, Velvary, Broumov, Mělník, Kutná Hora, and many other Czech towns. A large number of copies of the Holy Infant were exported. The Abbess of the Ursuline convent in Bratislava (Pressburg) M. F. Regedy had a sculpture of the Holy Infant placed in the choir chapel of her convent. More copies travelled to Germany (e.g. Buchau), to France (e.g. Paris), to Poland (e.g. Piekary), to Hungary and Austria, and later to Asian countries too (the Philippines, Vietnam, and China). In 1992 a copy of the Prague Holy Infant was handed over to Spain; thus the Holy Infant returned to its original homeland, even though in copy. The 'Little Praguer' will surely help unite the religious devotees of all countries where the national and political unity fails.

A GUIDE TO THE CHURCH
OF THE VIRGIN MARY
THE VICTORIOUS

On entering the temple, every visitor is attracted by the massive early Baroque façade. In the tympanum there is a motif of a star, reflecting the dedication of the church to the Virgin Mary (Stella Maris), and also the fact that the grounds had belonged to the Order of the Barefooted Carmelites, as a star was part of its sign. The window is covered with a wooden panel of a paiting of the Prague Holy Infant. Below the picture there is the coat-of-arms of the Spanish nobleman, the Imperial General and Knight of the Maltese Order Don Baltasar de Marradas at whose expense the façade, together with the musical choir, was built in 1644. The inscription below the insignia testifies to the fact: 'Out of gratitude end special reverence to St Theresa and her holy order, at his own expenses, he that bears these insignatia had the façade built and them set in it.' Part of the early Baroque sandstone portal forms a niche surrounded by twelve stars, in which there is a stone Madonna on the crescent, which was commissioned by the Baron Husmann in 1644 for 400 guilders, to be made as a replica of the gracious sculpture from 1626. The original sculpture is part of the altar in the right-hand chapel under the choir, together with the sculptures of God the Father in the upper part, and of SS Joachim and Anne by Jan Antonín Geiger from 1735-40. The same sculptor is the author of both the confessionals, in whose construction the wood-carver František Krafft co-operated. The reliefs in the altar depict the life of the Virgin Mary; the reliefs in the pendentives capture the Holy Fathers. The chapel was established in 1654 by the freeman Jan of Talmberk. Behind the entrance to the church there is a Baroque grill with the picture of a Marian sculpture. The opposite chapel of the Holy Rood (called the Talmberk Chapel) was built in 1654 at the expense of Vilém and Jan Arnošt, the freemen of Talmberk. The Baroque grill with a tiny picture of the Holy Infant of Prague shows the place where from 1656 to 1776 the Holy Infant was worshipped. The altar of the chapel adorned with reliefs of the Christological cycle, has a large cross with the Virgin Mary, St John the Evangelist, and a kneeling St Mary Magdalene below it. The re-

Alonso Sanchéz Coello,
Doña María Maximiliana Manrique de Lara
with the small Polyxena,
last quarter of the 16th century, detail,
Středočeská galerie,
Nelahozeves Castle

*Alonso Sanchéz Coello, Doña María Maximiliana Manrique de Lara
with the small Polyxena, last quarter of the 16th century, Středočeská galerie,
Nelahozeves Castle*

liefs in the pendentives depict the Evangelists. Below the choir there is also a stone sacred water basin which used to serve as baptistery in the former Lutheran church .

We can start the tour at the first left-hand altar. This aedicule altar of St Theresa of Ávila, decorated in black and gold, was made by Abraham Stoltz in 1668. The picture of St Theresa's Ecstasy was painted in 1752 by the Dresden painter Johann Georg Dietrich. The altarpiece of St Theresa is flanked by the sculptures of St John the Baptist and St Hieronymus, perhaps from Jan Antonín Quitainer's workshop.

The next altar — that of St John of the Cross — was established in 1669 at the Švihov family's expense, as also indicated by the coat-of-arms of this family depicted there. Set in the black and gold altar, the painting is of 'St John of the Cross Ascending to the Saviour' from 1669, by the court painter of the Bavarian Elector, Matěj Zimprecht. The mensa bears the picture of the Virgin Mary of Mantua on a gilt base, trimmed by a rich silver frame. At times, the reverence to this picture may have eclipsed that of to the Holy Infant. There is an interesting history to the picture, which is briefly captured in the reliefs on the base. According to a legend, the picture, hanging on a tree near the town of Matua, was shot at by a soldier. Blood spurted from the spot where the bullet hit, and then the rebounded bullet hit the shooter. The picture, painted on wood, was then kept in Mantua as miraculous. In 1626 Mantua, at the time occupied by French troops, surrendered to the Austrian army led by Count Annibale Collalto. The Count took the picture with him as war spoils to Graz,

and there he handed it to the widow Anna Felicita Stenzler of Grünberg to take care of. After the death of the Count the widow moved to Prague and in 1642 she gave the picture to her confessor P. Cyril of the Church of the Virgin Mary the Victorious in Malá Strana. The Mantovian picture was first worshipped by the members of the order in the cloister chapel, and in the times of the plague it was carried in processions (e.g. in 1680). On November 21, 1680, it was placed in the altar where, with a short interruption of 1700-17, it has remained. Similar to the Holy Infant, this picture was also adorned with many gifts, but these were gradually stolen. In the Virgin Mary's breast, where the bullet had hit, there is a crystal star with gold rays, set with Czech garnets. The star was presented by Countess Renata Slavata. The history of the picture and also of the miracles linked to it are described in the manuscript *Mantuanisch-Pragerisches Gnaden-Wölcklein Eliae-Geschichtsverfassung der Wunderzeichen, welche Gott durch, das Mantuanische-Mariae-Bild in den Kirchen deren Carmelitern in d. Königl. Kleiner Statt Prag gewürcket hat,* which contains records from the years 1626-1936.

Next to the altar a massive wooden pulpit is situated. Its roof is decorated with a sculpture of the prophet Elijah in a chariot of fire. In a niche below is a sculpture of the prophet Eliseus with his mantle billowing over his shoulders. Both sculptures are the work of J. L. Scheiermann from 1679. The architecture of the pulpit was done by M. Nonnenmacher. The front of the pulpit bears small pictures of the Carmelite's saints: St John of the Cross, St Theresa of Ávila and St Dionysius — all by Matěj Zimprecht.

Prague Holy Infant altar

The last altar on the Gospel side is that of St Simon Stock with a painting 'St Simon Stock Receiving the Scapular from the Virgin Mary', which was executed before 1720 by the Czech Baroque painter Petr Brandl, same as the picture of St John of Nepomuk in the upper part of the altar. Part of the altar are also three sculptures of popes, cardinals and archbishops who came from the Carmelite Order.

The High Altar was reconstructed into a symbolical triumphant arch in 1723 by Ferdinand Schor. The tabernacle is adorned with a fine gilt polychromous wood-carving of 'Angel Feeding Elijah in the Desert' and behind the throne of the Holy Sacrament there is a relief of Christ in Emmaus. Flanking the columns are large sculptures of the main patrons of the Carmelite Order: on the left the prophet Elijah and St Theresa of Ávila, on the right St John of the Cross and the prophet Eliseus. These can be ascribed to a follower of Matěj Václav Jäckel. Above the triumphant arch a large crown is situated and under that a copy of the White Mountain picture made in Rome by Robert de Longin; it is surrounded by the trophy.

Under the triumphant arch stands a Virgin Mary statue made in the second half of the 19th century by Jindřich Čapek. The former Carmelite choir is entered by gates adorned with the Carmelite emblem and curtains with the Johannite cross. In the monks' choir a beautiful painting of Elijah with the angel by Brandl was hung (now in the National Gallery of Prague) which had originally been placed in the refectory.

The back of the church is decorated with a painting by Matthias Mayer, whose subject matter is the help of the Virgin Mary in the Battle of the White Mountain. In the forefront we can see a kneeling Emperor Ferdinand II, Ferdinand III, King of Bohemia, and the Carmelite Dominic a Jesu with the Strakonice picture in his hand. In the second plane of the picture the Battle of the White Mountain is rendered. In the upper part the Virgin Mary and hosts of saints pray to the Holy Trinity for the victory of the Imperial Army. The benches of the monks' choir and other furnishings were commissioned by Prince Kamil Rohan to be adapted in a neo-Gothic style. The gift is recalled by the sculptures of two saints — SS Camilla and Adela — patrons of the prince and his wife, made by the sculptor Emanuel Max.

The altars on the Epistolar side are early Baroque in the main. Nearest to the choir is the altar of the Death of St Joseph. The painting in the altar, rendering St Joseph dying in the presence of the Virgin Mary and Christ, was painted in 1720 by Petr Brandl. He is also the author of the picture of St Anthony of Padua in the upper part of the altar. Flanking the altar stand the sculptures of the two saint Carmelites.

The most valuable treasure — the Prague Holy Infant — is kept in an altar of red and grey marble, made in 1776 by František Lauermann. The sculpture of God the Father in the upper part and those of St Joseph and the Virgin Mary were carved by Petr Prachner. The sculpture of the Holy Infant is housed in a glazed case of immense value, which together with the twenty little angels was made by the Packeni goldsmith family. The sculpture stands on a beautiful pedestal adorned with crystals, Czech garnets, and a large ruby in the shape of a heart.

Prague Holy Infant on the silver base

The altar of SS Joachim and Anne, which was commissioned in 1661 by the Countess Diettrichstein, exhibits the most beautiful picture within the church, titled 'The Prayer of SS Joachim and Anne'. As was the picture of God the Father in the upper part, it was painted in 1716 by Petr Brandl. The sculptures in the altar represent Pope St Theodore, the holy Bishops SS Andreas and Cyril. The mensas of all the altars bear the Maltese cross added by the Johannites during their administration.

The ceiling of the temple is decorated with frescoes depicting God the Father and the Imperial eagle with an inscription 'Hac praedante fides datur'. Next to it there is the Hungarian emblem and the Czech lion surrounded by the emblems of the Czech lands: Moravia, Silesia, and the Upper and Lower Lusatia, below which is written: 'Hoc certante conservatur.' The emblem of Malá Strana follows, then the Carmelite Order's sign, and finally a crown with a hand brandishing a sword (an allusion to the fact that they had spiritual administration in the army); above, there are eight stars and in the shield below the crown there is a cross with three stars. Under this sign, at the end of the passage there is an inscription: 'Hoc precante conservatur.' The meaning of the signs and inscriptions is: the Imperial eagle returns faith to the nations, the Czech lion confirms it by its fight against the Swedes, and the Carmelites spread the faith by their prayers.

Under the temple there are extensive crypts where the Carmelites and benefactors of the cloister are buried. Owing to favourable climatic conditions the remains of the dead are very well preserved even after hundreds of years.

The reminiscence of the last rites does not diminish the joy of spiritual encounter with the Holy Infant of Prague.

Jan Royt

THE ARCHITECTURE
OF THE CHURCH

At the turn of the 16th century construction activity in Prague was remarkably intense and varied. An Imperial commission was not in fact the most important one. The Emperor's architects designed a number of buildings for various other investors. In the last decade of Rudolf's rule the leading architect in the Emperor's service was Giovanni Maria Filippi, who had been called here from Rome. In March 1602 he became head of the Prague Imperial Construction Office. He seems to have worked on the design of the stately entrance to Prague Castle from Hradčanské Square. But out of the originally proposed more extensive project in 1613-14 only the monumental front of Matthias' Gate, in which the Baroque style entered Czech architecture, was brought to completion. As soon as the gate was finished, construction activity at Prague Castle came to a standstill and two years later Filippi was dismissed from the Imperial service for proven enrichment at the Emperor's expense.

Giovanni Maria Filippi was born in Dasindo near Trent. He probably trained in Innsbruck. His early work includes marble portals and church windows in his native Dasindo from 1586. For the next decade he worked in Rome. Filippi's activity in Bohemia is linked with artistically important deeds at the end of Rudolf's reign. Evidence exists of his other, unrealized projects, remarkable in their conception. He worked on a number of Imperial constructions outside Prague as well. Filippi was a creative spirit who could develop what he had learned in his native Italy — both from the theoretical works of Serlio and from the buildings by Ammanati, Vignolo, Pal-

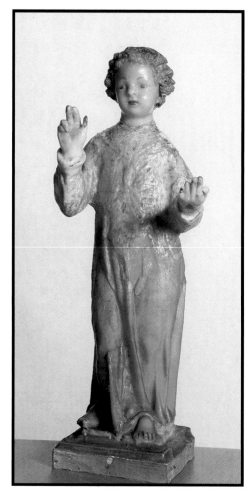

Prague Holy Infant without clothing, mid-16th century

ladio, and others — into lively compositions, but almost always tending to a Baroque expression. His church buildings exhibit this inclination inspired by the works of the Roman proto-Baroque, mainly by those of Giacomo della Porta, whose influence on the beginnings of Czech Baroque architecture was crucial.

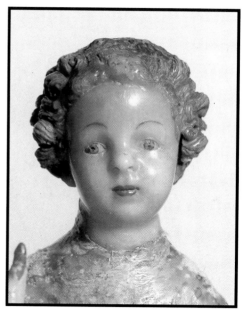

Head of the Prague Holy Infant in profile   *Head of the Prague Holy Infant*

The first of those buildings was the Lutheran Church of the Holy Trinity in Malá Strana, today the Church of the Virgin Mary the Victorious. Its construction was undertaken by the Germans of Hradčany and Malá Strana who settled in those parts of Prague in Rudolf II's time in large numbers. As early as 1597, the German speaking Lutherans applied for one of the Prague churches to be provided for their divine service, at least on Sundays and holidays, but their attempt failed. In Malá Strana they had to make do with a small chapel, quite inadequate to their needs and numbers.

The decree issued by Rudolf II on July 9, 1609, ensuring full religious freedom in Bohemia may have been an incentive for the Lutheran Germans to start their own constructional activity. Buildings of two large churches rose almost simultaneously in the course of the following years — one in Staré Město, one in Malá Strana — financially supported from abroad as well. Not many of the original written accounts of the construction of the Lutheran church in Malá Strana are extant. What we do know, however, confirms the idea that it was not a burghers' project only, for the rising temple was also to serve the aristocracy and the Lutheran members of the Emperor's court, same as the envoys of the German Lutheran lands and their retinues. Out of the aristocratic donators the most important personality seems to have been Henry Julius, Prince of Brunswick and Lüneburg, who since 1607 was a member of the Emperor's court, in the years 1607-11 lived in Malá Strana, and later moved to a newly-acquired house in Hradčany.

Holy Infant in the white robe

The foundation stone to the new church was laid on July 20, 1611; the not quite finished, yet usable church was consecrated on July 26, 1613. It needs to be said that the installation of the foundation stone did not necessarily mean the beginning of construction activity. On the contrary, in the Renaissance and Baroque periods, it was habitual to hold the celebration of the foundation stone at a rather advanced stage of construction — frequently on the premises of the roughly finished building. But the date of the dedication always meant the date of the beginning of worship, and thus it can be proved that at least the interior — the immobile furnishings and decorations — had been completed. Acquisition of the moveables for the interior (altars, pictures, sculptures, etc.), as with the completion of the exterior, could have taken yet much longer. In the case of the Holy Trinity Church this can be documented by the history of the altar commissioned for the interior by Prince Henry Julius of Brunswick and Lüneburg from the Saxon court architect Giovanni Maria Nosseni, which — completed as late as 1618 — had never been installed in the temple. The manuscript of the Carmelite monk P. Raymund, written in the late 18th century, with the use of an older chronicle describing the origins and history of the church, states that the original construction of the Lutheran temple was the work of a 'Catholic architect' and that the costs reached a staggering sum of 62 thousand Rhenish guilders. The sum itself supports the assumption that the construction must have started considerably earlier than 1611, and the building therefore did not come into existence in the course of two, but rather four or five constructional seasons, which would also better correspond to the size of the grounds.

The identification of the 'Catholic architect' (unnamed by the sources) with the Emperor's architect Giovanni Maria Filippi — as suggested by J. Zimmer — seems more than certain. It is proven by substantial similarities of the church in

Dress given, according to tradition, by Empress Maria Theresa in 1743

Malá Strana with other church constructions by Filippi. When staying in Italy in
1613, Filippi designed a collegiate temple
in Arco near his native town where he
came to fetch his family and take them to
Prague. There are far-reaching resemblances both in the general disposition and in
the details of the two church interiors, even
in the arrangement of the side spaces
flanking the chancels. In the exterior there

*The oldest dress made of silk velvet
from 1700*

is a striking motif of the volutes above the pillars in between the chapels adjoining the nave, and also the use of thermal windows. Identical, too, is the arrangement of the in-drawn entrance vestibules with the choirs adjacent to the main fronts. In its general features, the Arco church is only a larger variant of the Prague building. Since 1612, the Jesuit pilgrimage Church of Our Lady in Stará Boleslav had been built from Fi-

*Detail of the silver embroidery of the
dress illustrated on page 75*

Prague Holy Infant's crown

Dress made of blue brocade decorated with gold embroidery, mid-18th century

lippi's design, and its interior space and the general conception of the exterior closely follows that of the construction in Malá Strana. Partial differences are attributable to a further strengthening of the aspects of early Baroque monumentality in the temple of Stará Boleslav. The building was finished in 1623 by the architect Jacopo de Vaccani. After his dismissal from the Emperor's service, Filippi settled in Brno. He was called there by a letter of March 16, 1617, from Charles, Prince of Liechtenstein, who, same as Rudolf II, had ten years earlier been godfather at the baptism of the architect's son. For the Prince of Liechtenstein Filippi designed the church in Vranov near Brno, dedicated to Our Lady, which was built from 1617 to 1630 (with an interruption of the war years). The builder was Andreas Erna from Brno, and Filippi supervised the construction regularly. Even this church is a variant of the original compositional type.

Strikingly close resemblances of the four church buildings, out of which two are proved to be Filippi's by archival accounts, the exception of this type in Central Europe, its obvious Roman origin, and the quality of the execution – all speak for the assumption of them being the work of one architect. It is thus almost certain that Filippi is the designer of the Lutheran Church of the Holy Trinity in Malá Strana.

Its appearance that Filippi had originally proposed is evident in the plans kept in

Gold brocade dress with an embroidery of river pearls, second half of the 19th century

the Municipal Museum of Prague. Both the layout and the sectional view reveal that the size of the nave and of the present entrance space on the east side are identical with the original proposal. In reality the church was oriented in the opposite manner, though. East of the nave there was a square chancel with a tunnel vault, ending in a compressed semi-oval whose conch vault was divided by radial ribs. On the west side, the entrance with the choir was adjacent to the nave, set between the two proposed towers of the front. The views of the main and side façades, same as the drawing of the building in perspective, en-visage a main front which had never been executed in this way. It was to have two corner towers, with the central plane slightly receding. It is obvious that the general arrangement of the façade and its component architectural forms indeed follow the composition of the façade of the Roman church Sta Trinita dei Monti whose present form had been completed to the design by Giacomo della Porta in 1580—87. It exhibits an identical arrangement of the sections, the same motif of the large thermal window on the second floor in the central axis, and the execution of the campaniles on the upper floors of both the

Dress made of silk velvet with gold embroidery, river pearls, and Bohemian garnets, second half of the 19th century

towers, which are identical almost to detail. The campaniles are provided with specially shaped octagonal cupolas on low drums, with oval windows on the corner sides. Giacomo della Porta had already used this compositional element on the upper floor of the towers of St Anastasio dei Greci church in 1577. What is also interesting about the plan of the main front of the Prague building is the shape of the portal whose aedicule is formed by coupled Roman-Doric pilasters supporting moulded disjointed entablature and a segmented fronton with a disjointed base. This highly dynamic shape is an obvious variant of the aedicule of the central window on the first floor of the front of the Conservatori Palace in the Roman Capitol that had been added to the original façade of Michelangelo's by the architect Giacomo del Duca before 1603. The thermal and aedicule windows of the side façades of the church in Malá Strana are of a similarly evident Roman origin, and more instances of other models could be named from the circle of Vignola's followers. The general mass arrangement of the side façades of the Prague church is a variation of that of the Roman church of Sta Maria ai Monti, another work of della Porta's, finished in 1580.

In Central European architecture it was both the exterior and the intrior of the Lutheran church in Malá Strana that after 1600 was so innovative. The disposition and proportions of the main space, expli-

*Dress of coarse red cotton, embroidered with gold,
and with a cape made of genuine ermine, around 1900*

citly composed of the large and wide tunnel vaulted nave, and the clearly separated and delimited chancel, are in their basic qualities a contrast to the depth-oriented space of the Central European church buildings of the posthumous Gothic of the late 16th and early 17th centuries. This classical, clearly expressed conception of the space is again of obviously Roman origin. A particularly remarkable motif can be found in the articulation of the side walls of the nave. The niches of the shallow chapels cutting into them reduce the full entablature in the crown of the wall to sections above the Ionic pilasters. The archivoltes of the frontal joints of these chapels touch the axial conic keystones the lower edge of the cornice below the fully attached bottom of the vault. The Czech historian of architecture O. Stefan characterized this motif as explicitly Baroque. The mass modulation of the wall prevails over the arrangement determined by the forms of classical architectural morphology. The space of the two large spiral staircases in place of the originally proposed towers (today flanking the sides of the triumphal arch of the church) is of obvious Roman provenance, too. The staircases on the round plan circle the central clerestory, finished with four small supporting pillars. Since the buildings by Jacopo da Vignola this type of staircase had been an indisputable asset of Roman Mannerist and Baroque architecture.

Both the Czech temples built by Filippi — the one in Malá Strana and that in Stará Boleslav — were most important for the further development of Czech early Baroque sacred architecture. This type of ground plan was reflected in a number of variations over the following decades. One nave with the side niche chapels, the massive 'tunnel' space of the nave, and the shallow, centrally conceived chancel are not a variant of the ground plan of the Roman Il Gesù church, as has often been suggested in literature. The influence of both temples on the successive development of Czech early Baroque architecture undoubtedly had its ideological roots too, as both soon became Catholic temples of exceptional importance. The church in Stará Boleslav was the home of the Palladium of the Czech Lands and the most important pilgrimage place of its time; the one in Malá Strana — soon re-dedicated to the Virgin Mary the Victorious – a church linked with the Marian miracle of the White Mountain.

By a decree of October 24, 1622, Lutherans were banished from all the churches in the Czech Kingdom. They had to leave their church in Malá Strana too, and the building was sealed. Nearly two years later it was given to the Order of the Barefooted Carmelites for their newly established Prague cloister. Emperor Ferdinand II thus fulfilled part of his pledge by which he had promised to found two cloisters of the Barefooted Carmelites in his hereditary lands, Vienna and Prague. He had made this promise to the Order's General P. Dominic a Jesu Maria for the courageous conduct with which he had influenced the outcome of the White Mountain Battle. The Carmelites got possession of the church on September 7, 1624. The foundation charter of the cloister, though, is dated as late as August 26, 1625.

The sometime Lutheran Church of the Holy Trinity was a building of an architec-

Purple silk dress, first half of the 20th century

Holy Infant in a dress donated by an American, cape from the Philippines

Dress presented by the Carmelites from Tou-se-we village
near Shanghai, 1894

tural type and aesthetic standard that was preferred by the Barefooted Carmelites also in Italy. The Italian character of the church and its suitability for the Order's needs is mentioned in the cloister's chronicles as early as 1625. Nevertheless, for reasons of the Order's rules, certain constructional alternations of the church had to be undertaken. First of all, it was necessary to establish an extensive monk choir behind the main altar. With the existing situation of the building it was impossible to adjoin it to the chancel, at the time facing on the street. That is why the subsequent reconstruction included the change of the orientation of the building

Dress donated from Tou-se-we
near Shanghai, 1894, detail

J. J. Schmidt, votive picture from 1742,
sacristy of the Church
of the Virgin Mary the Victorious

Don Martín de Huerta. The foundation stone to both constructions was laid at the end of February 1626 which was the beginning of the construction season. The date thus probably agreed with the start of constructional activity, for only the foundation charter from July 1625 ensured the existence of the cloister legally. The construction of the monastery building and reconstruction of the church were prolonged – after the interruption of the war years 1631–32 – well into 1634. The arrangement of the interior followed the system of the original work by Filippi. The inconspicuous exterior of the chancel and choir with pointed arch windows, almost understated, was probably influenced by the building of the Carmelite church 'im Dau' in Cologne, finished in 1628. The Prague, Cologne, and Vienna convents formed in 1626 the basis of the newly established order province of the Holy Sacrament. When comparing today's situation of the church with the above mentioned plans for the originally proposed building, we find that the reconstruction retained the structure of the original church from its west frontal wall to as far as the section of the chancel (including the rooms adjacent to its sides). On the east side the termination of the chancel was pulled down and on the west side the choir and the entrance vestibule were removed and a deepened space of the new chancel and choir was adjoined to it. Furthermore, the side portal in the central section of the northern wall of the nave was blocked up and moved over to the outer wall north of the church. On the east side the reconstruction of the church resulted in a makeshift, yet plain gable wall with the main entrance.

and why the chancel and the choir were joined to the west of the nave. Simultaneously with these adaptations, the building of the cloister was being erected. Financial support for both constructions was provided by benefactors of the Order, mostly by the Emperor himself, and by the dreaded Imperial General, the Spaniard

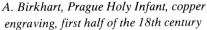

*A. Birkhart, Prague Holy Infant, copper
engraving, first half of the 18th century*

*J. Balzer, Prague Holy Infant, copper
engraving, second half of the 18th century*

It was only in 1636—42 that the spendid new main front was erected, out of the resources provided mainly by the dreaded army leader of the Thirty Years' War — General Don Baltasar de Marradas. The new front — the same as the original construction by Filippi — also makes an exceptionally important contribution of Roman inspiration to the Czech environment in the early development of the Baroque style. The new front was modelled on that of a Roman order church of Sta Maria della Vittoria, commmissioned by Cardi-

nal Scipione Borghese and built in 1624–25 from the design by the architect Giovanni Maria Soria. This very church (originally dedicated to St Paul) was the place where on May 8, 1622, the original of the miraculous and victorious picture of the Virgin Mary was transferred, on which glorious occasion the church was consecrated to the Virgin Mary the Victorious. The fact that the front of the Roman church was a decade later used as a consciously cited original in its Prague replica — maybe at the wish of the Barefooted Carmelites' rep-

*J. F. Fischer, copy of the Prague
Holy Infant in the former St Anne's
Convent in the Old Town of Prague,
copper engraving, around 1740*

resentatives — gives the Prague realization the 'vera effigie' significance, not so frequent in architecture, but very important for understanding the period. The author of the front is not known though. It is to be assumed, however, that its design came to existence in Prague, as the Roman original is imitated convincingly, yet with many slight changes due to the different dimensions of the structure and the architectural character of the former building, with which the new front forms a perfectly harmonized whole. Professional sources have only recently fully appreciated the outstanding quality of the front. The fact that the monumental façade recedes from the street line of one of Malá Strana's most frequented thoroughfares made it possible for an imposing space to be formed in front of it, the main compositional element of which is a massive terrace with a large axial entrance staircase. This space reinforces the aesthetic effect of the building in its immediate surroudings.

The constructinal development of the church was finished in 1669 by a relatively slim tower of the belfry roofed by a light bulb cupola. The two upper floors of the tower then executed were based on the outer walls of the two lower floors of the south tower (one of the two originally proposed by Filippi, but never built).

The Church of the Virgin Mary the Victorious has gone through a dramatic constructional development closely linked to the drama of history and its important events. During the period when it belonged to the Barefooted Carmelites' cloister in Malá Strana, the interior of the church was splendidly furnished and decorated with outstanding works of art and

Prague Holy Infant Giving Blessing

crafts made in the course of the Baroque period by prominent Prague artists. The artistic decoration sensitively complements the early Baroque space, and enhances the solemn genuineness and festive monumentality of this remarkable construction belonging to the most important examples of Central European early Baroque.

Mojmír Horyna

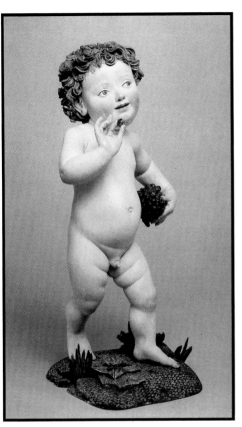

*Holy Infant of Salzburg, copper engraving,
18th century*

*Master of the Dangolsheimer Madonna,
Holy Infant with the Bunch of Grapes,
around 1462*

Angels, the Packeni workshop, Prague Holy Infant altar

SOURCES AND BIBLIOGRAPHY

SOURCES

1 Manuscript: *Pragerisches Gross und Klein,* kept at the parsonage of the Virgin Mary the Victorious, containing 296 pp. in all. Pages 1–122 are the work of the Prior of the Carmelite cloister P. Emerich a S. Stephano, pages 123–285 are by various authors from the years 1723–1936. Manuscript published in German: P. Emerich a S. Stephano, *Pragerisches Gross und Klein . . . ,* Prague 1749, in Czech translation under the title: *Pražské veliké i malé, to je výtah příběhů v milostech velikého, z vosku malého Jezulátka u karmelitánů,* Prague, Karel Hladký, 1749

2 Manuscript: *Mantuanisch-Pragerisches Gnaden-Wülcklein Eliae-Geschichtsverfassung der Wunderzeichen, welche Gott durch das Mantuanische-Mariae-Bild in den Kirchen deren Carmelitern in d. Königl. Kleiner Statt Prag gewürcket hat.* Containing entries from 1626–1936

BIBLIOGRAPHY

Gumpenberg, W. (translation into German by A. Sartorius): *Marianischer Atlas,* Prague 1717

Hammerschmid, F.: *Prodromus gloriae Pragenae,* Prague 1723

Bonani, J.: *Verzeichniss d. geistl. Ordens-Person* I, Nuremberg 1724

Leben des Gottseligen durch wunder thätigen Sig auf dem Weissen Berg bei Prag 1620 und andere Gnad und Wunderwürckungen berümtesten Diener Gottes Dominici von Jesu Maria, dess Barfüsser Carmeliter Ordens gewesenen: So zu Wien in Oesterreich in seiner Ordens Kirchen ruhet, mit vielen Gnaden Leuchtend, Regensburg 1729

Raymund P., *Rede auf den die feyerliche Uebertragung des Gnadenreichen Kindes Jesus bei den W.W.E.E. Vätern . . .,* Prague 1777

Schaller, J.: *Beschreibung der Residentzstadt Prag* II, Prague 1795

Votka, J. Kř.: *Pražské Jezulátko* (The Prague Holy Infant), in: *Blahověst* XXVI, Prague 1877

Párys, J.: *Kostel P. Marie Vítězné druhdy karmelitský* (The Church of the Virgin Mary the Victorious), in: *Památky archeologické* 3/1859

Beckovský, Fr.: *Poselkyně starých příběhů českých* II, III (Czech Stories of Ancient Times), published in Prague 1879 and 1880

Eckert, Fr.: *Posvátná místa královského hl. města Prahy* I (Sacred Places of the Royal City of Prague), Prague 1883

Krásl, J.: *Arnošt hrabě Harrach, arcibiskup pražský* (Arnošt, Count Harrach, the Archbishop of Prague), Prague 1886

Bortolotti, E.: *L'architetto della Chiesa collegiata di Arco,* in: *Ricordo del VII Congresso della Lega Nazione,* Trent 1900

De Rezende: *Můj flos sanctorum* (My flos sanctorum), Stará Říše 1914

Vondoerfer: *Eine Meissner Porzellanstatuette d. Prag. Jesuskindleins, Cicerone* XVII, Leipzig 1925

Ťoupalík, F.: *Milostné pražské Jezulátko* (The Gracious Holy Infant of Prague), Prague 1929

Schrieber, G.: *Strukturwandel der Wallfahrt*, in: *Forschungen zur Volkskunde* 16/17, Düsseldorf 1934

Articles in the review *Od Pražského Jezulátka* (The Prague Holy Infant), vols. I-III, Prague 1935—1938

Novotný, A.: *Pražské Jezulátko* (The Prague Holy Infant), Prague 1948

Lifka, B.: *L'enfant-Jésus de Prague*, in: *Les trésors de la broderie religieuse en Tchécoslovaquie*, Prague 1950

Wentzel, H.: *Christuskind*, in: *Reallexikon zur deutschen Kunstgeschichte*, vol. III, Stuttgart 1954

Stefan, D.: *Mluva pražské architektury* (Prague Architecture Speaks), Prague 1956

Blažíček, O. J.: *Sochařství baroku v Čechách* (Baroque Sculpture in Bohemia), Prague 1958

Stefan, O.: *Barokní princip v české architektuře 17. a 18. století* (The Baroque Principle in Czech Architecture of the 17th and 18th Centuries), in: *Umění* 7/1959

Němec, L.: *The Infant of Prague — The story of the holy image and the history of the devotion*, New York, Benziger Brothers inc., 1958

Franz, H. G.: *Bauten und Baumeister der Barockzeit in Böhmen*, Leipzig 1962

Poche, E.: *Prahou krok za krokem* (Prague Step by Step), Prague 1963

Joaha a Cruce, *Das Jesulein im Theresianischen Karmel*, Wil 1965

von Herzogenberg, J.: *Prag*, Munich 1966

Neumann, J.: *Petr Brandl*, catalogue to an exhibition, Prague 1968

Huber, A. K.: *Iberische Kulteinflüsse im Barock der böhmischen Länder*, in: *Die Königsteiner Studien* 15/1969

Neumann, J.: *Český barok* (Czech Baroque), Prague 1969

Zimmer, J.: *Iosephus Heinzius architectus cum antiquis comparandus*, in: *Umění* 17/1969

Zimmer, J.: *Zum Stil in der rudolfinischen Kunst*, In: *Umění* 18/1970

Hausscher, R.: *Jesuskind*, in: *Lexikon der christlichen Ikonographie. Hrsg. v. E. Kirschbaum S. J.*, vol. II, Rome-Freiburg-Basel-Vienna 1970

Svátek, J.: *Organizace řeholních institucí v českých zemích a péče o jejich archivy* (Religious Orders in the Czech Lands and their Archives), in: *Sborník archivních prací* XX, 2/1970

Krčálová, J.: *Italští mistři Malé Strany na počátku 17. století* (Italian Masters in Malá Strana at the Beginning of the 17th Century), in: *Umění* 18/1971

Krčálová, J.: *Poznámky k rudolfínské architektuře* (Notes on Rudolfinian Architecture), in: *Umění* 23/1975

Lietzmann, H.: *Die Deutsch-Lutherische Dreifaltigkeits-, die spätere Ordenkirche Sta Maria de Victoria auf der Kleinen Seite zu Prag*, in: *Zeitschrift für Kunstgeschichte* 40/1977

Krčálová, J.: *Die Kunst zur Zeit der Renaissance und des Manierismus*, in: *Die Kunst der*

Renaissance und des Manierismus, Prague 1979

Krčálová, J.: *Kostely české a moravské renesance. Příspěvek k jejich typologii* (Churches of the Czech and Moravian Renaissance and their Types), in: *Umění* 29/1981

Kotalík, J. T.: *L'architecture,* in: *Le baroque en Bohême,* catalogue to an exhibition, Paris 1981

Krčálová, J.: *Die rudolfinische Architektur,* in: *Leids Kunsthistorisch Jaarboek* 1/1982

Preiss, P.: *Italští umělci v Praze. Renesance, manýrismus, baroko* (Italian Artists in Prague. Renaissance, Mannerism and Baroque), Prague 1986

Zenetti, L.: *Das Jesuskind. Verehrung und Darstelung,* Munich 1987

Vilímková, M. — Líbal, D.: *Umění renesance a manýrismu — architektura* (Art in the Period of Renaissance and Mannerism — Architecture), in: *Praha na úsvitu nových dějin,* Prague 1988

Remešová, V.: *Milostné Pražské Jezulátko* (The Gracious Holy Infant of Prague), Prague 1988

Naňková, V.: *Architektura 17. století v Čechách* (Architecture in Bohemia of the 17th century), in: *Dějiny českého výtvarného umění* II/1, Prague 1989

Horyna, M.: *Urbanistický a architektonický vývoj* (The Development of Architecture and Urban Planning), in: *Historie a současnost Prahy 1,* Prague 1989

Niños Jesús, scultore policrome dalle Collezioni Reale di Madrid, Milan 1989

Hilger, H. P.: *Das Jesuskind mit Weintraube,* Munich 1991

THE HOLY INFANT
OF PRAGUE

THE HOLY INFANT OF PRAGUE
Text by Josef Forbelský, Jan Royt, Mojmír Horyna
Translated by Kateřina Hilská
Photographs by Karel and Ladislav Neubert
Graphic design by Miroslav Pechánek

Sixth English edition 2004

© AVENTINUM s.r.o., 2004
Printed in the Czech Republic
ISBN: 80-903284-5-8